HIDDEN
CORNWALL

INTRODUCTION

I've loved researching this book. I grew up in Cornwall and have lived here most of my life, yet there were so many places I'd never visited. Having founded the wearecornwall.com website, I set out on a mission to venture further than the familiar haunts I know well to explore some of the county's other hidden spots. It's been a fascinating journey and one that I'm delighted to be able to share within the covers of this book.

I'd like to thank the friends and family who have accompanied me on my trips, often at very short notice. It's lovely to be able to compare notes about an experience and I always love the camaraderie and fun. My dog Daisy is invariably with me these days to join in the adventure too – she especially enjoys letting me know what she thinks of local tea rooms!

Finally, great thanks need to go to Anna Corbett, my editor and publisher at Tor Mark, for all her support and encouragement, and Briony Vercoe for her excellent design work. What a team!

Sue Bradbury

 SAT NAV

 PARKING

 WALKING

 DISABLED ACCESS

 DOG FRIENDLY

 OPENING TIMES

 CAFÉ

 PUB

 SHOPPING

 TOILET FACILITIES

CONTENTS

MORWENSTOW

Morwenstow is a real North Cornwall treat. Situated just about as close to the Devon border as you can get, the small hamlet leads to an impressively magnificent seascape with precipitous rocks and seemingly inaccessible beaches.

This is a place made famous by a rector who left his mark in more ways than one. Regarded by many as a delightful eccentric who loved dressing up in bright colours, the Reverend Stephen Hawker was a prolific writer and poet who penned the words to the county's much-loved anthem **Trelawney** and published a significant number of books.

Inspired by the magnificent scenery around him, he built a hut out of driftwood on the cliff top and used it as a writing refuge. Somewhere he could sit, contemplate and put pen to paper. Hawker's Hut, now the National Trust's smallest property, is little more than a makeshift shed with spectacular views around three quarters of a mile from the church. You can walk to it, sit on the bench-like seats and share the experience of past literary greats like, Alfred Lord Tennyson and **Water Babies** author Charles Kingsley who, as the vicar's guests, once relaxed there too.

Bookish and characterful, Reverend Stephen Hawker was also a compassionate man who did his best for his parishioners and those in peril from the sea. When the **Caledonia**, a 200-ton ship from Scotland, came to grief on Lower Sharpnose Point in 1842, he ensured that all those who drowned were given a decent burial in the churchyard - the ship's figurehead still marks their mass grave today. Similarly, when the **Martha Quayle**, from Liverpool, lost its mast and began to founder in 1863, Hawker helped save the whole crew by alerting the nearby Appledore lifeboat.

Wander down the steeply sloping path from Rectory Farm through trees towards the church, enjoy the coolness of the ecclesiastical building and a heritage that goes back centuries before emerging into fields and the coastal path beyond. Take note, too, of Hawker's former vicarage with its church-tower-shaped chimneys and, on the horizon, the unmistakable shape of unspoilt Lundy Island.

- Hawker's Hut -

- Widemouth Bay -

DID YOU KNOW?

Reverend Hawker is credited with introducing Harvest Festivals.

The first service took place in the church on 1st October 1843.

i USEFUL
Information

- SAT NAV: EX23 9SR

- There is free parking next to the church entrance and tea room.

- The walk to Hawker's Hut is gentle but good footwear is recommended.

- Dogs should be on a lead in fields with livestock in them and where the path gets close to the cliff edge.

- There are no public toilets but there is a very good café and a pub.

✚ WHAT
Else?

GCHQ Bude, a secret spy base perched on the cliff top between Morwenstow and Coombe. Twenty-one different sized satellite dishes point at different angles towards the sky, continually alert for internet-based messages that might pose a threat to our country's security. According to former US intelligence analyst-turned-traitor Edward Snowden, America's National Security Agency has paid millions of pounds into GCHQ's coffers to keep the Bude base at the top of its game. Two rows of barbed wire fencing and CCTV monitoring keep the curious at bay, but the space-like antennae are nonetheless an intriguing landmark on an otherwise largely unblemished stretch of outstandingly scenic coast.

 TIME
For tea

Rectory Farm Tea Rooms are an absolute delight. First opened in the 1950s, they are still run by the same family and continue to achieve award-winning ratings. Menu treats include homemade scones, cakes, quiches, chutneys and mouth-watering soups using recipes passed down through generations – as well as proper Cornish pasties and, of course, Cornish cream teas (jam first!) www.rectory-tearooms.co.uk

? WHAT'S
Nearby?

- Stratton, an ancient market town near Bude and the scene of the battle of Stamford Hill in 1643. The Tree Inn on Fore Street, SAT NAV: EX23 9DA, used to be the Manor House – birthplace of Anthony Payne who, at 7ft 4in, was known as the Cornish giant.

- St Swithin's church in Launcells, described by poet Sir John Betjeman as 'the least spoilt church in Cornwall'. The fifteenth century building has original floor tiles made in the Barnstaple potteries and exceptional Tudor bench ends. SAT NAV: EX23 9NQ

- Widemouth Bay. Key features include one and a half miles of golden sand, some of the best surf in Cornwall and a range of watersports. SAT NAV: EX23 0AQ

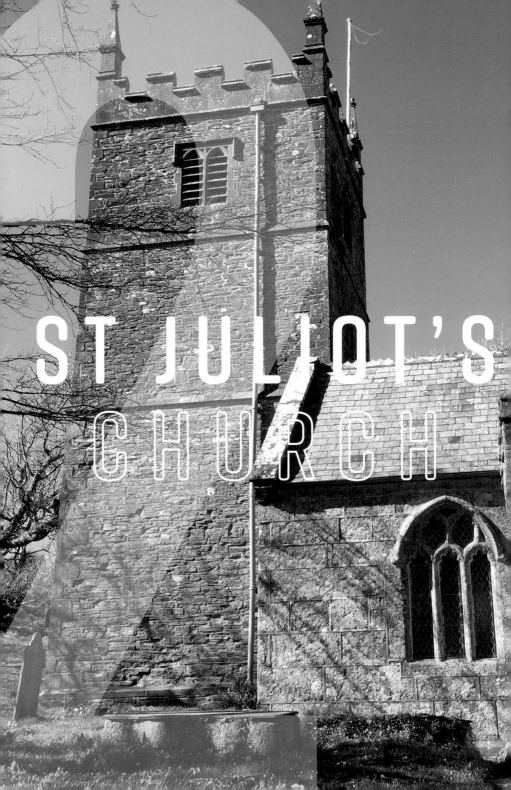

ST JULIOT'S
CHURCH

As the famous author Thomas Hardy discovered, **St Juliot's** isn't a place you're likely to stumble upon by accident. Having worked in architecture for fourteen years, Hardy had travelled down from Dorset on 7th March 1870 because the church was in an extremely dilapidated state and he'd been tasked with helping to restore it. The journey involved a pre-dawn start and was reportedly a nightmare. When he finally arrived at the rectory in the evening, he was met, not by the rector who was in bed with gout, but by his sister-in-law Emma Gifford.

Describing Emma later as the 'young lady in brown', the budding novelist — who had just posted the manuscript of **Desperate Remedies** which was to become his first published work — was instantly smitten. Over the next few days he spent his time 'drawing and measuring' in the church, whilst also getting to know Miss Gifford, who had moved to St Juliot when her sister married the vicar. By the time he returned to Dorset, Hardy wrote in his poem **When I set out for Lyonesse** it was 'with magic in my eyes'.

Mutual attraction turned rapidly to love in a place that was transformed from 'irremediable dilapidation' to a much-enhanced church, that officially opened on 11th April 1872. In September that year, Hardy read the lesson at a service and, during his stay, received a letter offering him more architectural work in London. Should he accept or take a gamble and write full-time? With Emma's support, he refused the former and chose the latter. His next novel **A Pair of Blue Eyes** drew largely on his experiences at St Juliot's and, after finishing **Far from the Madding Crowd**, the couple married on 17th September 1874.

- *Valency River* -

For the next 38 years they lived in Dorset, but what seems to have begun as a romantic union of minds, with a shared appreciation of books, poetry and nature, gradually dwindled into a much less than happy relationship. Maybe Emma felt the frustration of knowing that her own literary talent was as nothing compared to her husband's genius or perhaps they both needed Cornwall and the beautiful backdrop of St Juliot to rediscover the feelings that its setting had inspired.

When Emma suddenly died in November 1912, Thomas Hardy made his own final pilgrimage to the church where they met. He organised a memorial for Emma on the wall of the north aisle and wrote his **Poems of 1912-13**, which many regard as being amongst the finest literary examples of love and regret in the English language.

DID YOU KNOW?

St Juliot's is located in Valency Valley. In 2004, the Valency River caused severe flooding in Boscastle - resulting in huge structural damage, national headlines, but thankfully no loss of life.

i USEFUL
Information

- SAT NAV: PL35 0BT

- There is a parking area in front of the church entrance.

- Dogs on leads are welcome.

- The nearest café is Boscastle Farmshop.

- Shops and toilet facilities are available in nearby Boscastle.

- Boscastle Harbour -

TIME
For tea

Nearby **Boscastle Farmshop** has an award-winning café that boasts wonderful panoramic views and excellent food. Much of it is locally sourced. Sit by a window or outside on one of the benches to make the most of the fabulous surroundings. For those wanting some exercise, the South West Coast Path is just a stone's throw away. SAT NAV: PL35 0HH
www.boscastlefarmshop.co.uk

? WHAT'S
Nearby?

- Valency Valley, a secluded, peaceful retreat that's home to plenty of wildlife and is one of North Cornwall's few wooded areas.
www.nationaltrust.org.uk/boscastle/features/valency-valley

- Tintagel Castle, possibly the legendary Camelot. Situated in a stunning setting, visiting this age-old ruin with its fascinating history is a must.
www.english-heritage.org.uk/visit/places/tintagel-castle/history-and-legend/description

- Slaughterbridge, the supposed site of King Arthur's last battle. A sixth century inscribed stone is said to mark the spot where he met Mordred for the decisive battle of Camlann, which brought an end to the fellowship of the Round Table. SAT NAV: PL32 9TT

WHAT
Else?

Boscastle itself – a beautiful historic harbour village managed by the National Trust. First settled in the 12th century, it's a picture-postcard type of place that's perfect for a wander. There's a very good Visitor Centre and the Museum of Witchcraft and Magic houses the world's largest collection of witchcraft-related artefacts and regalia. Definitely worth a look.

PORT QUIN 3

ocated on the North Cornish coast four miles west of Port Isaac, **Port Quin** is often referred to as the 'village that died'. Why? Because one Sunday night during the nineteenth century, legend has it that all the men in the small coastal community broke the Sabbath by going out to fish, got caught in a violent storm and drowned. Unable to continue putting food on the table without the income their husbands provided, the widows were forced to abandon their homes to the elements and leave with their children. If true, it's a desperately sad tale of tragedy and loss and one that was probably all too common in this part of the world little more than a century ago.

The earliest mention of Port Quin is in 1327 when Laurence de Porquin took his name from the village. Pilchards were the main form of livelihood and the size of what were once fish cellars - and are now mainly holiday cottages - tends to suggest that the catches were often good. The natural harbour was also used as a minor trading base for shipping coal, manure, stone and lead to Wales and the granite used to build nearby St Endellion Church was transported here from Lundy Island.

There's definitely a feel of travelling back in time as you take the narrow country lane in St Endellion that leads to Longcross Victorian Gardens and the turning to Port Quin. On the left as you start to descend to the cove is the entrance to Doyden Castle. Built in 1830 as a retreat for local **bon viveur** Samuel Symons and said to be the venue for much partying and gambling in its time, it's a folly that the National Trust now rents out to visitors. The building is clearly visible from the coastal path on the other side of the beach and can best be described as a rather strange looking crenellated tower with arched windows and Gothic archways in a glorious seaward facing position. Apparently the ample wine bins in its cellar are a lasting testament to the feasting and general excesses that once took place there.

Port Quin itself nestles between Kellan Head and Doyden's Point – a sheltered inlet that some say is the place that Viking longboats once came ashore, though sadly there is little evidence for this.

- Port Quin Cove -

Situated in an area of outstanding natural beauty, it's quiet and peaceful with a small beach, soaring cliffs and some excellent walks. Look beyond the dramatic seascape, though, to discover a past that hasn't always been so tranquil.

- Polzeath -

- Port Isaac -

DID YOU KNOW?

Port Quin is in the parish of St Endellion, which hosts some very popular classical music festivals. Poet Sir John Betjeman, who loved the area too, wrote: "St Endellion! St Endellion! The name is like a ring of bells."

 USEFUL
Information

- SAT NAV: PL29 3SU

- There is a National Trust car park with a ticket machine in the village.

- Dogs are banned on the beach from Easter Day to the 1st October.

- There are no cafés or shops in the hamlet.

- The nearest public toilets are in Port Isaac.

TIME
For tea

The Terrace Tearooms in nearby Port Isaac serves delicious cream teas on vintage bone china. Located above the village, the main car park is only a short walk away. **SAT NAV: PL29 3SE**

WHAT
Else?

Port Isaac is just a short drive further along the coast from Port Quin. Globally famous for providing the authentic Cornish backdrop in the recent popular TV series **Doc Martin**, it is still a working fishing village with plenty of character and charm. Top chef Nathan Outlaw runs a couple of excellent restaurants there – one has two Michelin stars, the other offers seafood plates at reasonable prices.

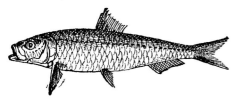

WHAT'S
Nearby?

- Delabole Slate Quarry, where Delabole slate is quarried. You can take a tour from Monday to Friday, excluding bank holidays. www.delaboleslate.co.uk
SAT NAV: PL33 9AZ

- Polzeath, a trendy and upmarket small coastal village with a lovely sandy beach, that is very popular with surfers and swimmers – although care needs to be taken with rip tides. **SAT NAV: PL27 6SS**

- Port Gaverne, a pretty, sheltered cove around the corner from Port Isaac that has rock pools, caves and views.
SAT NAV: PL29 3SQ

ST ENODOC CHURCH

t's normally quite easy to spot a church with a tower, but that isn't the case with **St Enodoc**. Surrounded by a tall hedge, sand dunes and a golf course, you have to look for the path that leads from the nearby village of Trebetherick. Follow it and you'll discover a granite building with a crooked spire, unique charm and a special place in Cornish history.

Originating from the twelfth century and famous for being the last resting place of Sir John Betjeman, St Enodoc is also known as 'Sinkininney Church'. That's because, over the centuries, it's been almost buried by sand for long periods of time. To hold a service, legend has it that one vicar led his parishioners through a hole in the roof. Whether or not that story is true, it is known that the church had to be dug out from the dunes during the nineteenth century and was then completely restored. There was even a new bell for the tower, claimed from the wreck of an Italian ship that had foundered on the notorious Doom Bar sand spit at the mouth of the Camel Estuary.

Trebetherick, near Rock, is where the Betjemans once spent their annual holidays. An only child and, by all accounts, a lonely one, John clearly loved the place. Accompanied by his favourite teddy bear Archibald and far away from his main home in London, he made friends with the local children, played by the water's edge, made 'long barefoot climbs to fetch the morning milk', discovered small coves and took part in treasure hunts. "Childhood," he said when referring to his time in Cornwall, "is measured out by sounds and smells and sights, before the dark hour of reason grows."

The church itself has a wonderfully restful feel. On one of the walls is a memorial to the three crew lost at sea, when the sail training ship **Maria Assumpta** sank on rocks at Rump Point, in 1995, whilst preparing to enter Padstow, and another pays tribute to John Betjeman's father Ernest. The lead-lined twelfth century granite font is also worthy of interest.

Outside, pause at the upper end of the cemetery and look towards stunning Daymer Bay with its wide sandy beach, historic Brea Hill with its Bronze Age tumuli to your left and, separating Daymer from the small cove of Greenaway to your right, Trebetherick headland, where shipwrecked remains can still be seen on the foreshore.

For Betjeman, Trebetherick wasn't just a safe haven in boyhood but a lifelong second home that inspired many poems. After a long, successful career that culminated in the honour of becoming Poet Laureate, he died in the village and is buried at St Enodoc. You can see his headstone immediately to the right of the entrance gate.

- Daymer Bay -

USEFUL
Information

- SAT NAV: PL27 6LD – beware, though, this will take you to St Enodoc golf course. Your best plan is to head for Daymer Bay car park and walk from there.

- You'll be walking across a golf course to get to the church so, sensible shoes are recommended. The route may not be easily accessible for those with impaired mobility.

- Dogs on leads are welcome.

- The church is open daily from 7.30am until dusk.

- There are café, shop and toilet facilities at Daymer Bay car park.

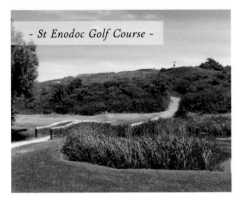

- St Enodoc Golf Course -

WHAT
Else?

Rock – an attractive coastal village on the Camel Estuary that has become a popular sailing, five-star eating and spot-the-famous centre. Known for expensive second homes and well-heeled clientele, it's a great place to people watch. There's also a handy passenger ferry to Padstow.

TIME
For tea

Why not treat yourself to a sumptuous afternoon tea at **The St Moritz Hotel** in Trebetherick? Be prepared for a feast – with sandwiches, scones, cakes and speciality teas and coffees included. The views from the seaside restaurant and bar are stunning but you'll need to book 24 hours in advance. SAT NAV: PL27 6SD
www.stmoritzhotel.co.uk

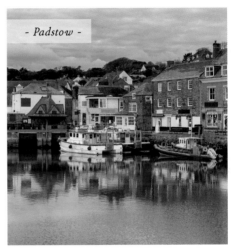

- Padstow -

WHAT'S
Nearby?

- Prideaux Place, a grade 1 listed Elizabethan house in Padstow, which has been home to the same family for 400 years.
SAT NAV: PL28 8RP

- Polzeath beach, a haven for surfers that is known for its wealthy – and sometimes royal – visitors. SAT NAV: PL22 6TB

- Brea Hill, a wonderful natural vantage point from which to survey the Camel Estuary and waves crashing onto Doom Bar.
Map Ref: SW92847714

Most of us have heard of Gretna Green, but how many people know that Cornwall had its own romantic bolthole — St Catherine's Church in **Temple**, a tiny hamlet close to the A30 on Bodmin Moor?

Described in 1584 as 'lying in a wild wastrel, exempted from the Bishop's jurisdiction where many a bad marriage bargain is yearly slubbered up,' weddings could be performed there without banns or licences. As such, it was the perfect place to run to if parents or family didn't approve or unexpected pregnancy threatened scandal. 'Slubbered up' means to do something imperfectly or coarsely. Hardly an appealing turn of phrase, but one that certainly indicates society's attitude then to couples desperate for, whatever reason, to exchange vows quickly.

That feeling of escaping the world, with all its violence and sometimes brutal judgement, is still there when you pass through the gate, wander down the path bordered by gravestones and enter St Catherine's time-worn walls. Peaceful and picturesque, with history oozing from every nook and cranny, it's still a place to pause, reflect and revive.

The original twelfth century church had a much happier reputation. Built by the Knights Templar who owned the land, it was a place that offered hospitality and safety to travellers. Distinctive for the red cross on a white background that they traditionally wore on their cloaks, Templar knights were treated like heroes for almost two centuries, before losing their power and influence when the Holy Land was lost. The Order was officially disbanded by order of the Pope around 1307 but, as recent films and novels prove, the legend lives on.

Visit St Catherine's Church today and you'll see the famous red cross in some of the stained glass windows. Pilgrims crossing the moor would have once found refuge here, looked after by religious men who fed them and gave them shelter. Hundreds of years later, temporary sanctuary was also offered to those looking to give a church blessing to relationships some might have considered unwise.

DID YOU KNOW?

The saying 'send her to Temple Moors' was used to describe women who were considered outcasts and needed to correct their ways.

ℹ USEFUL
Information

- SAT NAV: PL30 4HW

- You can park on the road immediately outside the churchyard.

- Accessible for those with impaired mobility – please note there is a narrow path from the road to the church.

- Dogs on leads are welcome.

- The church is open during daylight hours.

- There is no café, shop or toilets.

- Colliford Lake -

© Martyn Hall

☕ TIME
For tea

Jamaica Inn, made famous by the Daphne du Maurier novel of the same name, is a short drive further along the A30. Serving food throughout the day – including cream teas – it was first built as a coaching inn in 1750 and boasts one of the biggest collections of smuggling artefacts in the UK. SAT NAV: PL15 7TS www.jamaicainn.co.uk

❓ WHAT'S
Nearby?

- Hawk's Tor, 7 miles north east of Bodmin and 307 metres above sea level. A good place to include on a moorland hike.
  NGR: SX 1412 7555 (SX 1417 55)

- Altarnun, a pretty village with whitewashed, slate-roofed cottages and a babbling stream, just a stone's throw from the A30. The vicar of Altarnun played a major role in Daphne du Maurier's novel **Jamaica Inn**. SAT NAV: PL15 7SJ

- Colliford Lake Reservoir, the largest lake in Cornwall. Picnic areas, walks and an important site for birdlife.
  www.swlakestrust.org.uk
  SAT NAV: PL14 6PZ

➕ WHAT
Else?

Warleggan. A tiny hamlet a few miles further on that is said to have inspired author Winston Graham when he was looking for a name to give his evil banker in Poldark. Described as one of the most remote areas in Cornwall, the 200 or so residents clearly have a sense of humour. Below the sign that announces their village is another saying that they are twinned with Narnia. Maybe their wardrobes really do have a lion, a witch and a Mr Tumnus in them!

HIDDEN
CORNWALL

ST IVES

REDRUTH

6

PENZANCE

HELSTON

DING DONG

MINE

DING DONG MINE 6

Eliza Jane Hall was just 17 when she died in an horrific accident at **Ding Dong Mine** in West Cornwall. As a bal maiden, she was one of the many young women in Cornwall who worked hard above ground in the mines. Like her friend Alice Ann Stevens, she was employed in the stamp mill where small lumps of ore were crushed into sand-like material. She had probably been labouring from the age of about 10 and could have expected to stop when she got married. Sadly, that was never to be. Fooling around during a meal break, she climbed onto a stationary wheel used to haul materials up from underground. Alice, who was washing her hands at the time, shouted at her to get down but, as the wheel began to move, Eliza excitedly declared 'I will go round'.

Seconds later, her dress got caught in the machinery, crushing her right leg and extensively breaking her left foot. Medical help was quickly at hand but the poor girl died from her injuries the same day. She was buried at Gulval.

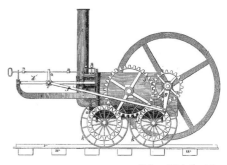

- *St Michael's Mount* -

Mines were very dangerous places and Ding Dong's distinctive chimney on windswept Penwith Moors stands as a reminder of many such lives and losses. Getting there means walking over land that has probably changed little over millennia, vulnerable to weather extremes and dramatic in terms of views. Mine workers would have trudged the muddy, gorse-bordered paths on a daily basis, passing the Bronze Age Mên-an-Tol en route.

The holed stone is said to be responsible for miraculous cures thanks to a Cornish pisky guardian and legend has it that, if a woman passes backwards through the hole seven times at full moon, she will soon become pregnant.

Richard Trevithick worked as an engineer at Ding Dong in 1797 and it was there that he first developed a high pressure engine capable of raising ore and waste rock from the mine. When the legal representatives of rival engineers threatened to take him to court for infringing their patent, this giant of a man frightened them off with his own threat of throwing them down the Ding Dong shaft. Four years later, Trevithick's famous passenger-carrying steam locomotive puffed its way into the history books.

© Trevithick Society

Standing proud, tall and remote in its bleak moorland setting with views for miles around, Ding Dong Mine is an intriguing sentinel to the past whose hidden depths run deep.

Photographs © Hilary Daniel

USEFUL
Information

- SAT NAV: TR20 8XX

- Head for TR20 8XX and park in the layby. Parking in the layby is free but space is limited.

- Robust, waterproof footwear is highly recommended.

- The circular route to Ding Dong Mine, the Mên-an-Tol and Nine Maidens Stone Circle takes about 2 hours.

- The route is gently undulating, without any very steep inclines.

- There are no dog waste bins.

- There are no roads, so your dog can stay off-lead all the way.

- There are no public toilets.

WHAT
Else?

The Nine Maidens Stone Circle, which is otherwise known as Boskednan. Despite the name, it's thought that there were originally 22 stones, but there are now only 11 and not all of them are standing upright. The site is Neolithic and believed to have been used for pagan rituals more than 4000 years ago.

TIME
For tea

The Tinners Arms in Zennor was built in 1271 for the masons who built the local church. Stone floors, log fires, low ceilings and a lovely outdoor area make it a perfect place to enjoy good food in a beautiful coastal setting. SAT NAV: TR26 3BY
www.tinnersarms.com

WHAT'S
Nearby?

- Lanyon Quoit, 3 standing stones with a large flat capstone, weighing 13 tons, resting on top of them – hence the Quoit's alternative names Giant's Table or Giant's Tomb. Situated in a field on the right as you approach the parking area for the Ding Dong Mine walk, it's an impressive sight – once you've managed to spot its location from the road. SAT NAV: TR20 8NY

- Madron enjoys stunning views of Mount's Bay. Its church once served the Penzance district and, between the village and the rocky outcrop behind it known as Madron Carn, is a well-known holy well (TR20 8SD) that's reputed to have miraculous healing powers.

- Chun Castle is an impressive Iron Age hill fort on the opposite side of the road to the Ding Dong Mine walk. Roughly circular, you can see the remains of several houses, two 3-metre high stone walls and an external ditch. The views are far-reaching. SAT NAV: TR20 8PX

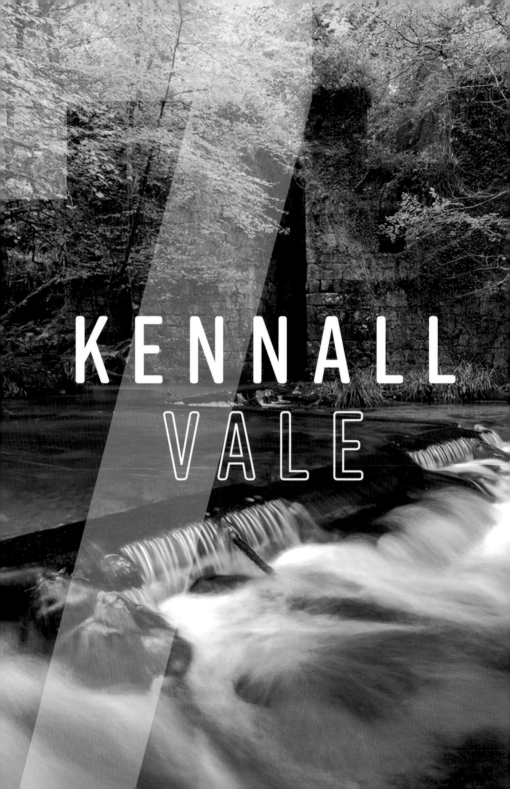

S tep into **Kennall Vale** Nature Reserve on the outskirts of Ponsanooth and discover a magical woodland with an intriguing, explosive past.

Now a peaceful, beautiful place to wander, Kennall Vale was once a hive of industry. Whilst today birdsong and the sound of running water provide a gentle, beguiling audio backdrop, the noise of yesteryear was far more jarring and invasive. So much so that huge numbers of trees were planted to help absorb the daily cacophony and occasional ear-splitting blasts. Why so much loud activity? Because this was the site of the most successful gunpowder works in Cornwall.

In its early nineteenth century heyday, around 50 men worked out of 56 buildings in Kennall Vale. Harnessing the power of the fast-flowing River Kennall that falls rapidly through the valley, they were busy making about 4000 barrels of gunpowder each year – mostly for local mines and quarries but some for worldwide exportation. It was a very successful business but one that brought many obvious hazards. In 1826, local resident Elizabeth Rutter visited what was known as the Mixing House with a basket of hot roast potatoes for the three men working there. The well-meant gesture had terrible consequences. A spark from the freshly cooked food ignited the highly unstable mixture being worked on and it exploded, killing Elizabeth, one of the labourers and severely injuring the others.

Other such tragedies occurred with grim regularity over the subsequent decades, until the invention of gelignite and dynamite brought about a decline in gunpowder production. In 1910 its manufacture at Kennall Vale ceased completely. Granite quarrying continued for a while but, when that ended too, nature took over.

Designated a Cornish Mining World Heritage area, Kennall Vale is managed by Cornwall Wildlife Trust. Paths created for horse and cart provide a circular walking route that meanders past sunny glades and old walls covered in ivy and moss, before plunging down to the impressively thundering river. Throughout the year dippers and grey wagtails can be seen along the river with the occasional visit from a kingfisher at the quarry pool. In spring a few bluebells, wood sorrel and wood anemones occur but the valley is arguably at its best in autumn, with plenty of colour. Look for fungi, including the porcelain fungus on the moss-covered branches of beech trees and keep an eye out for small creatures, such as the incredibly colourful larva of the pale tussock moth which occurs here.

Photo opportunities exist at every twist and turn and children, dogs and adults will love the adventure.

Photographs © David Chapman

DID YOU KNOW?

Gunpowder is made out of saltpetre, sulphur and charcoal – all of which had to be brought to Kennall Vale from outside Cornwall. Also known as 'black powder', gunpowder was invented by the Chinese as far back as 850AD.

i USEFUL
Information

- SAT NAV: TR3 7HJ

- The entrance to Kennall Vale is on Cot Hill and parking on the road is not advisable. It's best to park in Ponsanooth village and walk up.

- The tracks and paths can get very muddy and wet so wear sensible shoes or boots.

- Wheelchair users can access some, but not all of the paths.

- Dogs are welcome.

- Kennall Vale is always open to visitors.

- There are no toilets, cafés or shops.

✚ WHAT
Else?

Ponsanooth may be a village that many people just drive through on their way to either Falmouth or Redruth, but it's well worth looking at. For several hundred years it was known for its wool manufacturing as well as its gunpowder works but, in 1843, the five storey woollen factory burnt down. When visiting, take the time to look around the local shop. In December 2013, it was destroyed by floods but, thanks to the local community who came together to restore it, it's now a thriving business selling a wide selection of Cornish produce.

 TIME
For tea

The **Olive Grove Bistro** at Barras Moor Farm in Perranarworthal is a 5 minute drive away. Set in the lovely surroundings of Cornish Garden Nurseries, they serve a great tea that's available all day. It includes homemade scones and a delicious range of homemade cakes, some of which are gluten-free. If you want something more substantial, there are very good breakfast and lunch menus. Visit: www.theolivegrovebistro.co.uk for more details. **SAT NAV: TR3 7PE**

- Gwennap Pit -

© Gwennap Pit

? WHAT'S
Nearby?

- Enys Estate, an historic house and gardens that are well known for their magnificent display of bluebells in the spring. People come from far and wide to see them. www.enys.co.uk **SATNAV: TR10 9LB**

- Stithians Lake, ideal for taking part in a variety of water sports, camping, enjoying a snack or simply experiencing some lovely inland scenery on foot. www.swlakestrust.org.uk/lakes-and-facilities/the-lakes/stithians-lake **SAT NAV: TR16 6NW**

- Gwennap Pit, an open air amphitheatre made famous by John Wesley, the founder of Methodism. Part of the Cornish Mining World Heritage Site. **SAT NAV: TR16 5HF**

ST CATHERINE'S
CASTLE

ST CATHERINE'S CASTLE 8

S t Catherine's Castle sits at the mouth of the Fowey Estuary and it's not hard to imagine why it was built. Positioned on a promontory looking out across the English Channel, it's the perfect place to keep watch for enemy ships. At the time of its construction, Henry VIII had upset Rome and the Catholic world by insisting on divorce from Queen Catherine. Invasion was a real possibility so the King ordered more coastal defences. Local landowner Thomas Treffry obliged by building St Catherine's and, further down the coast, St Mawes Castle.

The fort was never used in anger — neither in Tudor times when it came into being nor during the Second World War when anti-aircraft guns were positioned there. Today it's a ruin that's conserved by English Heritage. Entry is free and the views across to Polruan, down the river to Fowey and over to St Austell Bay and the Roseland Peninsula are simply breathtaking.

People started living in the area during Medieval times – attracted by Fowey's proximity to the Channel and the ships sailing past. Piracy, smuggling and intrigue were certainly not uncommon and a kind of mob law was said to prevail. In 1457, the French attacked the town but, thanks to Dame Elizabeth Treffry who quickly rallied her men in her husband's absence, the foreigners are said to have been repelled with molten lead poured from the top of Place House.

The Treffrys have lived in Fowey for more than 600 years and Place, with its high walls and distinctive towers, is still their private home.

Thomas Treffry, the ancestor who built St Catherine's Castle, lived there for 54 years from 1509. Unlike his great aunt Dame Elizabeth, he didn't have to fight invaders at his own front door, but did end up spending a lot of his own money reinforcing local defences – a fact which he was keen to point out to Henry VIII's right-hand man, Thomas Cromwell, in 1536. No reply appears to have been recorded. Whilst the fort may have diminished Thomas' resources, it has become a wonderful legacy. Stand beside walls that are up to 4 feet 6 inches thick and marvel at a stunning panorama which, during the summer, includes a splendid assortment of boats.

- Fowey Estuary -

- Polkerris -

- Fowey -

DID YOU KNOW?

St Catherine's Castle is just off The Saints' Way – a long-distance footpath which follows the route that early Christian travellers would have taken when making their way from Ireland to Europe.

i USEFUL
Information

- SAT NAV: PL23 1JH

- The walk from Readymoney Cove car park is about ¾ mile.

- The walk to the castle may not be suitable for those with impaired mobility.

- Dogs on leads are welcome.

- Entrance to the castle is free and it is always open to visitors.

- The nearest café, shop and toilets are at Readymoney Cove.

- For more information, visit: www.english-heritage.org.uk/visit/places/st-catherines-castle

✚ WHAT
Else?

Readymoney Cove has a small sandy beach, which faces south east. Sadly you won't find cash growing on trees there – its name derives from the Cornish Porth Mundy, meaning mineral house cove. Daphne du Maurier rented Readymoney Cottage for a few years during the Second World War and wrote **Hungry Hill** there.

☕ TIME
For tea

The **Rashleigh Inn** at Polkerris opens directly on to a sheltered beach not far from Menabilly, the inspiration for Daphne du Maurier's Manderley in her most famous novel **Rebecca**. Snuggle up by the pub's log fire or enjoy the terrace seating. Lovely homemade food – from sandwiches to steaks. SAT NAV: PL24 2TL
www.therashleighinnpolkerris.co.uk

- King Doniert's Stone -

❓ WHAT'S
Nearby?

- King Doniert's Stone, two richly carved pieces of a 9th century Celtic cross. Managed by Cornwall Heritage Trust and free to see. SAT NAV: PL14 6EG

- Trethevy Quoit, a well-preserved and impressive Neolithic 'dolmen' burial chamber. There are five standing stones, with a huge capstone on top. SAT NAV: PL14 5JY

- Fowey, a lovely historic waterside town that has inspired many artists and writers. Daphne du Maurier and Sir Arthur Quiller-Couch among them. SAT NAV: PL23 1ET gets you to the main town car park.

S et high above Lostwithiel, with far-reaching views across the Fowey valley and lush, ancient woodland, Restormel Castle is an impressive sight. Not just because of its position — spectacular as that is — but also because of its perfectly circular shape.

It must have been quite an engineering feat to build it around 1100 when there were no cranes or lorries available to help ease the burden of transporting tons of stone from the river far below. To then follow a design that requires no external angles (apart from those in the square gate tower entrance), must have been a challenge. The result, though, was an aesthetically-pleasing fortress, which boasted some grand chambers, including a Great Hall, a keep and a chapel.

The Cardinham family were its first owners and occupants, but in 1264 it was seized without a fight by Simon de Montfort at a time when there was a lot of civil unrest. Not long afterwards Restormel was back in Cornish hands. Isolde de Cardinham gifted it to the newly created Richard of Cornwall, the King's brother, and from that day to this it has retained royal connections, becoming part of the Duchy of Cornwall estate from 1337 onwards.

Unlike many Cornish fortifications, the castle did see action – once during the English Civil War. Around 30 Parliamentarians were using it as a garrison when, on the 21st August 1644, Royalist Sir Richard Grenville and his troops attacked. The Parliamentarians were easily routed and the King's men re-claimed ownership. A century later, the castle was in ruins.

Now looked after by English Heritage, Restormel Castle is a poignant, impressive reminder of a past that relied on turrets, moats and very thick walls for defence. Wander through the remnants of its chambers, breathe in the history and admire a far-reaching vista from its ramparts that still includes vast swathes of countryside and woodland, with the ancient town of Lostwithiel some way below. As a building and location, the castle and its grounds are a delight to explore.

- Lostwithiel -

DID YOU KNOW?

In 1846 the British royal family visited the castle. They travelled on their yacht, the *Victoria and Albert*, which was moored on the River Fowey.

i USEFUL
Information

- SAT NAV: PL22 0EE

- There is a good-sized free car park next to the entrance.

- Accessible toilets are available on site. Visitors with limited mobility are advised to telephone ahead to arrange for appropriate access.

- Dogs on leads are welcome.

- The castle is open daily from 10 - 5pm.

- There are picnic benches and a gift shop with a vending machine that sells hot and cold drinks.

- For prices and visitor information, go to www.english-heritage.org.uk/visit/places/restormel-castle

 TIME
For tea

The award-winning **Duchy of Cornwall Nursery café** offers a good range of snacks, light meals and delicious Cornish cream teas in a tranquil, beautiful setting that looks out towards the Fowey Valley and Restormel Castle. Much is justifiably made of the locally-sourced food and drink.
SAT NAV: PL22 0HW
https://www.duchyofcornwallnursery.co.uk/the-cafe

? WHAT'S
Nearby?

- The Old Duchy Palace, Lostwithiel. Built in 1292, it's a Grade 1 listed heritage building that has recently been completely refurbished. https://princes-foundation.org/project/old-duchy-palace SAT NAV: PL22 0BS.

- Lostwithiel Museum. Housed in what used to be The Corn Exchange, the museum's collections include domestic objects, craft and agricultural tools, ceramics, medals and minerals. www.lostwithielmuseum.org SAT NAV: PL22 0BW.

- The medieval bridge in Lostwithiel which has spanned the River Fowey for seven centuries. www.lostwithiel.org.uk

✚ WHAT
Else?

Lostwithiel is an ancient stannary town that dates back to the 12th century. Historic appeal combines with great creativity — resulting in Cornwall's best collection of antique shops, a very popular farmers' market and an events calendar that includes Lostfest, a vibrant one-day arts, crafts and music festival that has really taken off.

CARNGLAZE

CAVERNS

Hidden by glorious woodland and a couple of miles off the main A38 near St Neot, **Carnglaze Caverns** is not somewhere you stumble upon by accident.

As the county's only slate mine, it has a fascinating history stretching back centuries. Slate is usually quarried and long before the nearby road was built, Loveny Valley, where Carnglaze is situated, was used for that purpose. Deep mining on the site began in the 1700s to find better quality stone. Being underground meant the men could work in all weathers so they went in at river level and gradually went up — back-filling with their waste material in the process (like an early form of recycling).

That meant they didn't need ladders or scaffolding — an altogether safer way of mining slate than was the case in North Wales, where a main cause of death was falling from great heights.

Carnglaze no longer produces slate but has, instead, been transformed into a visitor destination with four enchanting acres that allegedly boast fairies, a lovely woodland walk, glorious views and an underground experience that has a magic all of its own.

Tours are self-guided unless you book for a group — meaning you can often get the vast spaces to yourself. The first of those is the Rum Store — so-called because it was requisitioned by the Navy as a place of safe-keeping for the famously strong spirit. You can now also view a comprehensive mineral collection, mined and quarried in the South West.

A flight of 60 steps takes you down to the next level and the remaining two chambers. Atmospherically lit to showcase the rock formations and with occasional waxwork figures to illustrate how the miners dug out the slate. There is a baby pool that creates the illusion of being far shallower than reality (it's actually two metres deep and not the blue-green colour it appears). The pièce de résistance is the **Cathedral Chamber**; inside there is a small lake that is illuminated in different ways and includes rocky outcrops on which weddings are often held.

- Bodmin Moor -

© Visit Cornwall - Matt Jessop

- Golitha Falls -

 USEFUL
Information

- SAT NAV: PL14 6HQ

- There is free parking on site.

- The temperature is a constant 10° underground so a jumper and sensible footwear are recommended.

- Specific areas of the gardens and the lower chambers have limited access for people with impaired mobility and wheelchair users. The car park, ticket office and an adapted toilet all have wheelchair access.

- Dogs on leads are welcome in all outdoor areas – biodegradable doggy bags are available from the ticket office.

- Opening times: Monday-Saturday 10 - 5pm.

- An on-site refreshment area has vending machines selling hot and cold drinks and snacks. There is also a shop selling gifts, crafts and jewellery.

- For further information and ticket prices, visit www.carnglaze.com

WHAT
Else?

There's a tranquil woodland walk at Carnglaze, which boasts a stunning sea of bluebells in spring. The zig-zag pathways take you through a terrace garden and the so-called Enchanted Dell to the top of the valley and back. Along the way are hand-crafted signs indicating interesting natural features like fox holes and other flora and fauna.

TIME
For tea

You can buy light refreshments on site and enjoy your own picnic at one of the tables provided. Alternatively, **Inkie's Smokehouse BBQ** is in the Golitha Falls car park. An absolute gem of a café, it's award-winning, very good value and extremely dog-friendly. Make sure you take cash though – Inkie's doesn't accept cards but does do PayPal. **PL14 6RX**

WHAT'S
Nearby?

- St Neot, a small village with an interesting church known for its medieval stained glass windows. **SAT NAV: PL14 6PA**

- Golitha Falls **SAT NAV: PL14 6RU**, a National Nature Reserve and an officially designated Site of Special Scientific Interest (SSSI), thanks to its woodland flora. The river drops 90 metres along the floor of the gorge – resulting in a series of spectacular waterfall cascades.

- Bodmin Moor – wild, magnificent and a great place to walk.

KINGSAND &
CAWSAND

Overlooking Plymouth Sound, the only thing separating **Kingsand** from **Cawsand** is a small stream that these days goes virtually unnoticed. Insignificant as it might seem, however, that stretch of running water was, for centuries, the boundary between Devon and Cornwall. You can still see today what used to be the border on the front of one of the picturesque cottages, set against a blue-painted wall, the old demarcation line is black and the house itself is appropriately named Devon-Corn.

The conjoined villages are a delight to wander around, with their narrow streets leading down to small sandy beaches and far-reaching views across Plymouth Sound. There's a regular foot passenger ferry from Cawsand to Plymouth Barbican for those wanting to take to the water and a good selection of cafés, art galleries and quirky shops for those who prefer to remain land-based.

Whilst Kingsand and Cawsand are historic, scenic gems set against a backdrop of lush woodland that descends steeply to the sea below, their location on Rame Peninsula places them squarely in what is often referred to as 'Cornwall's forgotten corner'. It's all too easy for visitors to the county to bypass the area as they drive further west and for day trippers to seek out more familiar hotspots – yet the long narrow strip of headland jutting out into the English Channel has some fascinating history and memorably beautiful views.

Given their coastal location, it's unsurprising that Kingsand and Cawsand boast a past that is inextricably linked to both fishing and smuggling. Many of the tunnels reputedly used to bring in contraband goods have been sealed up but the unevenly shaped walls of homes, fish cellars and inns built hundreds of years ago tell secret tales of their own.

It was in the 10th century that the Anglo Saxon king Athelstan decreed a county division that saw Cornwall begin in Cawsand. In 1844 Devon was finally pushed back to the other side of the Tamar – meaning, of course, that when eating a cream tea in Kingsand, it's no longer acceptable to spread the cream first!

© Mount Edgcumbe

PRIVATE
NO ENTRANCE

DID YOU KNOW?

During World War II, a large number of fairly basic wooden chalets were built along the Whitsand Bay coastline by Plymouth residents wanting to escape their city's bombing. Now hugely sought-after for their position, they can change hands (when the rare opportunity arises) for hundreds of thousands of pounds.

i USEFUL
Information

- SAT NAV: PL10 1NA (car park)

- There are well-signed long-stay, pay and display car parks in both Kingsand and Cawsand.

- Suitable for wheelchair access.

- Restricted access for dogs on Cawsand Beach from Easter to October. Kingsand Beach is dog-friendly all year round.

- Village facilities include cafés, shops and toilets.

✚ WHAT
Else?

Plymouth has long been an important maritime asset. To help protect it from possible invasion, a series of fortifications and a road to connect them were built from Cawsand to Tregantle above Whitsand Bay in the 1860s. One of these was Polhawn Fort, which once housed a small gun battery that was never used in anger and is now one of the UK's most popular, exclusive-use wedding venues. Little wonder given its magnificent, seaward-facing location.

 TIME
For tea

The Old Bakery in Cawsand dates back to 1760 and is just a stone's throw from the sea. Sourdough bread is baked on the premises every day from scratch – using 100% organic ingredients. A great place for homemade breakfasts, lunches, cream teas, snacks and artisan takeaway pizzas.
SAT NAV: PL10 1RD
www.theoldbakery-cawsand.co.uk

❓ WHAT'S
Nearby?

- Mount Edgcumbe House and Country Park. Set in magnificent gardens, the estate is open to the public. SAT NAV: PL10 1HZ
www.mountedgcumbe.gov.uk

- Antony House, a superb early 18th century mansion that is now owned by the National Trust. SAT NAV: PL11 2QA
www.nationaltrust.org.uk/antony

- Rame parish church. First consecrated in 1259 and situated close to Rame Head, it famously has no electricity and is lit entirely by candles. SAT NAV: PL10 1LG

Cover Image: **Warleggan**
Title Page Image: **Restormel Castle**
Introduction Page Image: **Pont Pill, Fowey**

If you enjoyed 'HIDDEN CORNWALL' you may also like these...

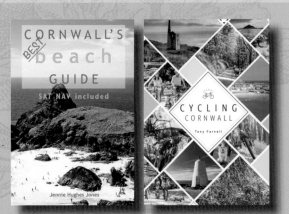

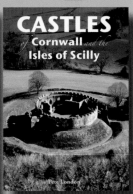

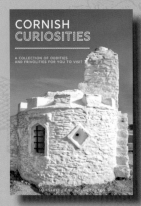

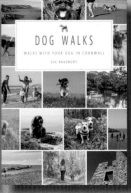

For information on all titles published by Tor Mark, please visit www.tormark.co.uk

TOR MARK

Published by Tor Mark,
United Downs Industrial Estate,
Redruth, Cornwall TR16 5HY

www.tormark.co.uk

Published 2019

ISBN 978 0 85025 495 2

Text © Tor Mark
Images © Adobe 2019, © Aerial Cornwall,
© Brusheezy.com, © Carnglaze Caverns,
© Carolin Coward, © David Carvey,
© David Chapman, © Gwennap Pit,
© Hilary Daniel, © Martyn Hall,
© Matt Jessop, © Mount Edgcumbe,
© Shutterstock, © Sue Bradbury,
© Tor Mark, © Trevithick Society,
© Visit Cornwall

Printed and bound in Great Britain
by Cambrian Printers